Dorothea Lange

PHOTOGRAPHER WITH A HEART

By Sara McIntosh Wooten

To my dearest friend, J.B.W.

For information contact:

Mondo Publishing
980 Avenue of the Americas
New York, NY 10018

Visit our website at www.mondopub.com

Printed in China

09 10 11 12 13   9 8 7 6 5 4 3 2 1

ISBN 978-1-60201-995-9

Design by Herman Adler

Photography and Quotation Credits:
Every effort has been made to trace the ownership of all copyright materials in this book and to obtain permission for their use.

Photography Credits: Front Cover: The Granger Collection, New York; 1: © Rondal Partridge; 4: Unknown, Oakland Museum of California, Lent by John Eaglefeather Dixon; 8: © Bettmann/CORBIS; 12: © Condé Nast Archive/CORBIS; 14: Dorothea Lange, American, 1895-1965 © The Dorothea Lange Collection, Oakland Museum of California, City of Oakland. Gift of Paul S. Taylor; 17: The Granger Collection, New York; 19: Dorothea Lange, American, 1895-1965 © The Dorothea Lange Collection, Oakland Museum of California, City of Oakland. Gift of Paul S. Taylor; 21 (left): Dorothea Lange/Collection of John and Lee Dixon; 21 (right): Compliments of Sunset Magazine; 22: Dorothea Lange, American, 1895-1965 © The Dorothea Lange Collection, Oakland Museum of California, City of Oakland. Gift of Paul S. Taylor; 23: Dorothea Lange, American, 1895-1965 Maynard Dixon & Sons-Dan & John? © The Dorothea Lange Collection, Oakland Museum of California, City of Oakland. Gift of Paul S. Taylor; 25: © Hulton Archive/Getty Images; 29: © Dorothea Lange/National Archives/Getty Images; 31: Gift of David and Marcia Raymond in honor of their father, Paul Raymond © Oakland Museum of California, courtesy of The J. Paul Getty Museum, Los Angeles; 35: © CORBIS; 36: courtesy of The J. Paul Getty Museum, Los Angeles; 37: © Bettmann/CORBIS; 39: The Granger Collection, New York; 41: © Dorothea Lange/ ImageEnvision.com; 42: © Rondal Partridge; 44:© Imogen Cunningham Trust; 46: The Granger Collection, New York; 48: © Dorothea Lange/ ImageEnvision.com; 50: © Time & Life Pictures/ Getty Images; 51: © CORBIS; 53: © CORBIS; 54: Dorothea Lange, American, 1895-1965 © The Dorothea Lange Collection, Oakland Museum of California, City of Oakland. Gift of Paul S. Taylor; 57: © Dorothea Lange/ ImageEnvision.com; 59: Dorothea Lange, American, 1895-1965 © The Dorothea Lange Collection, Oakland Museum of California, City of Oakland. Gift of Paul S. Taylor; 60: © Rondal Partridge

Quotation Credits: Pages 6, 7, 13, 28: Reiss, Susan. "Dorothea Lange: The Making of a Documentary Photographer," an interview with Dorothea Lange. Regional Oral History Office, University of California, Berkeley, 1968. Page 9: Partridge, Elizabeth. *Restless Spirit: The Life and Work of Dorothea Lange*. New York, Viking, 1998. Pages 18, 32, 38, 40: Doud, Richard K. Interview with Dorothea Lange. Washington, D.C. Archives of American Art, Smithsonian Institution, May 22, 1964. Pages 20, 26, 30, 43: Meltzer, Milton. *Dorothea Lange: A Photographer's Life*. Syracuse, NY: Syracuse University Press, 2000. Page 24: Coles, Robert. Essay in *Dorothea Lange: Photographs of a Lifetime*. New York, Aperture Foundation, 1982. Pages 45, 61: Partridge, Elizabeth, ed. *Dorothea Lange: A Visual Life*. Washington, D.C., Smithsonian Institution Press, 1994. Page 58: Ohrn, Karin Becker. *Dorothea Lange and the Documentary Tradition*. Baton Rouge, LA, Louisiana State University Press, 1980. Back Cover: Brainy Quote. http://www.brainyquote.com/quotes/authors/d/dorothea_lange.html

Contents

Portrait of Dorothea Lange, circa 1930

CHAPTER 1
Invisible

Dorothea Margaretta Nutzhorn was born on May 26, 1895. She was the first child of Joan Lange and Henry Nutzhorn. The family lived in Hoboken, New Jersey. Little did Joan and Henry know that Dorothea would become one of the greatest photographers of the twentieth century.

When Dorothea was seven years old, she became sick with a disease called polio. She had a very high fever. Every muscle in her body ached. After many days her fever broke. But the muscles in Dorothea's right leg had stopped growing. She would walk with a limp for the rest of her life.

Dorothea could no longer run and play as she'd done before. Children made fun of her. They called her "Limpy." Dorothea felt that her mother was ashamed of her, too. Joan would whisper "walk straighter" into her daughter's ear when other people were around.

"No one who hasn't lived the life of a semi-cripple knows how much that means. I think it was perhaps the most important thing that happened to me. I've never gotten over it and I am aware of the force and power of it,"

Dorothea later said when reflecting on having polio.

When Dorothea was 12 years old, her father suddenly left. He would never return. Dorothea never spoke of this loss. She would never understand why her father went away.

Life quickly changed for the Nutzhorn's. Dorothea's mother found a job at a New York City library. It paid well. However, soon the family had to move. They went to live with Joan's mother, Grandma Sophie.

Life with Grandma Sophie was a big change for Dorothea. The woman was often moody and very loud. She was never afraid to speak her mind. However, Dorothea discovered that she and her grandmother were very much alike. They both were strong-willed. Each also understood and enjoyed the artistic side of life. Grandma Sophie taught Dorothea the importance of doing her best. Years later the woman's passion for excellence would carry on in her granddaughter's work.

Dorothea went to middle school in New York City. She and her mother would wake up very early each morning and ride on a ferryboat to Manhattan. Then Joan would walk Dorothea to school. After that Joan would head to the library.

In New York, Dorothea walked side by side with people from all cultures. The city was much louder than Hoboken. Trains clanked as they traveled on tracks above the pavement. The calls of street peddlers filled the air. Dorothea heard many different languages, too. Her nose picked up the scents of exotic foods. She was now exposed to many new things.

"

I very early remember that my grandmother told me that of all the things that were beautiful in the world, there was nothing finer than an orange, as a thing. And I knew what she meant, perfectly,"

Dorothea said when speaking about her grandmother.

New York City's Lower East Side, where Dorothea went to school, was home to many European immigrants during the early 1900s.

Dorothea had always been a good student. But she faced new challenges in the seventh grade. Her school had close to 3,000 students. Most of them were immigrants. These students didn't speak English. Dorothea couldn't understand their language. She now knew what it felt like to be an outsider.

Dorothea walked to the library after school each day. She waited there while her mother worked. She enjoyed browsing through the books on the shelves. Dorothea would study the photographs in the books. She would see something beautiful in every picture.

Some nights Joan worked late. On these evenings Dorothea walked to the ferryboat by herself. She strode through the dangerous streets of New York City. Dorothea was scared. But she knew she had to control her fear.

" I can turn it on and off. If I don't want anyone to see me, I can make the kind of face so nobody will look at me, "

said Dorothea Lange, describing how she could become invisible to others.

Dorothea walked with a blank face. She didn't look at anyone. The girl never let her fear show through her greenish blue eyes. The girl learned to make herself invisible. Dorothea didn't know then that this skill would help her later in life.

Soon Dorothea was in high school. By this time her independent spirit had taken over. She enjoyed visiting the city's many museums. Often her best friend, Fronsie, joined her. Dorothea also liked to watch people on the streets go about their everyday activities. She was no longer afraid of the big city.

In 1913, Dorothea graduated from high school. Joan wanted her daughter to become a teacher. So Dorothea enrolled in a teacher's school. But soon she announced her true career choice. "I want to be a photographer," she told her family.

CHAPTER 2
A Bold Choice

In the early 1900s, photography was thought of as a "man's" career. Joan wondered how Dorothea would be able to succeed as a photographer. The girl had never even taken a picture with a camera. Dorothea understood her mother's concerns. But this didn't discourage her from pursuing her dream. When Dorothea had an idea in her head, she would go after it. And going after photography was just what she did.

One day Dorothea strolled down New York City's Fifth Avenue. She paused in front of a store window. Portraits were in the display. The photographs were the most beautiful she'd ever seen.

Arnold Genthe took the portraits. He was one of New York City's most well-known portrait photographers. Soon Dorothea met with Genthe. She convinced the photographer to hire her to work in his studio.

Arnold Genthe, who taught himself photography
while living in San Francisco, gave Dorothea her
first photography lessons.

Little by little Genthe taught Dorothea about
photography. First he taught her how to print proofs.

Then he showed her how to use a small brush and dark ink to touch up the portraits. Finally he taught Dorothea how to frame the final images. Dorothea picked up many valuable photography lessons from Genthe.

Working at the photography studio introduced Dorothea to the world of the rich and famous. She worked closely with Genthe's wealthy customers. Dorothea set up lights for portrait sessions. She observed the careful way Genthe framed his portraits. She also noticed how her teacher was able to bring people's internal beauty to life on film.

> That was a look into a world I hadn't seen. . . . The most miraculous kind of living,
>
> said Dorothea Lange about working with Arnold Genthe.

Eventually Dorothea felt she had learned all she could from Genthe. So she left Genthe's studio to work at a larger one. Soon she had the opportunity to conduct her first portrait session.

Despite having jitters, Dorothea's first portrait session turned out well. The owner of the studio was very

In 1927, Dorothea took this portrait of her mother, Joan.
(photograph called *Untitled (Portrait of Joan Bowley,
Dorothea Lange's mother)* is pictured)

impressed with Dorothea's work. This success helped Dorothea build her confidence as a photographer. It also led to more opportunities to photograph customers.

Dorothea was now even more serious about becoming a photographer. She took a photography course at Columbia University. She also bought her first camera. To practice portrait photography, Dorothea took pictures of her family. She built a darkroom in her backyard. The room was a special place where she could develop her photographs.

Soon Dorothea wanted to open a studio of her own. The 22-year-old was also eager to move out of her grandmother's home. Dorothea decided that she would travel around the world. She wanted to observe people from all cultures and photograph them.

In January 1918, Dorothea said goodbye to her family. Then she and her friend, Fronsie, set out on their adventure. The two girls left from New York City. They traveled by ship to New Orleans, Louisiana. From there they took a train to California. On May 18th, they finally arrived in San Francisco. Already they had been traveling for almost four months!

Dorothea and Fronsie had come so far. But soon their grand plans fell apart. On their first day in San Francisco, their money was stolen. But this didn't bring down their spirits. The two young women planned to earn their money back. By the end of the next day, both of them had jobs.

Dorothea's new job was at a photography counter in a San Francisco department store. She took customers' film and sent it to a laboratory to be developed. Once the pictures came back, she would put the final prints into frames.

Dorothea's new job put her in contact with many well-known artists in the San Francisco area. Among them were photographer Imogen Cunningham and etcher Roi Partridge. With their help, Dorothea joined a local camera club. Her plans to travel around the world had been ruined. However, Dorothea soon realized that fate had been on her side.

CHAPTER 3
A Fresh Start

Dorothea Lange, circa 1920

Six months passed. Dorothea was now ready to open a photography studio. A local business man lent Dorothea $3,000 to start her studio. With the money,

she rented space in San Francisco and opened her business. The studio soon became a meeting place for the city's community of artists. Painters, writers, and other photographers would gather there. They would drink tea and dance to music. But most times Dorothea was hard at work in her darkroom.

> "It was a good little studio, a fine little studio,"
>
> Dorothea once said when asked about her studio.

By this time Dorothea's friends and customers all knew her as Dorothea Lange. "Lange" was her mother's maiden name. Dorothea would use this name instead of "Nutzhorn."

Dorothea's business grew rapidly. She worked in her darkroom late into the night. Her portraits quickly became popular. All well-to-do people in the San Francisco area wanted their picture taken by Dorothea.

In order to do well, Dorothea knew she needed to take very special pictures. She was very professional. Dorothea would interview her customers before a

Shown here is a portrait that Dorothea took in her San Francisco studio in 1930. (photograph called *P. Wallen Portrait, San Francisco* is pictured here)

portrait session. This was how she got to know them. The interviews also helped customers become more comfortable with Dorothea. In this way, Dorothea was able to capture the true spirit and personality of everyone she photographed.

> "I seriously tried, with every person I photographed, to reveal them as closely as I could,"
>
> Dorothea later said about her work as a portrait photographer.

One day Roi Partridge, a good friend of Dorothea's, came by Dorothea's studio. He brought a visitor with him. It was the artist Maynard Dixon. The newcomer was dashing. The man was tall and thin. He had piercing dark eyes and a dark mustache. He was dressed like a cowboy. Dorothea thought that her new visitor looked mysterious.

Dorothea was fascinated by Maynard's stories of childhood. When he was young, he had suffered from asthma. He, too, had grown up as an outsider. Dorothea realized that Maynard loved the American Southwest. His paintings depicted the lives of Native Americans, ranchers, and cowboys.

Dorothea quickly fell in love with Maynard, even though he was 20 years older than she was. Within six months, they were married. They moved into a tiny house. Their new home was close to both of their studios. Dorothea's business was now booming.

SEPTEMBER 1934   10 CENTS

SUNSET

As well as painting, Maynard also illustrated covers for books and magazines.

Maynard Dixon, circa 1923

Taking photographs of Native Americans was just the
beginning of a new kind of portrait photography for
Dorothea. (photograph called *Girl and Cornstalk* pictured)

She was known as the best portrait photographer in San
Francisco. Maynard's paintings were selling very well, too.

The two often traveled to the Southwest. Sometimes
they stayed there for weeks. Maynard would paint
the scenery. Dorothea would photograph the Native
Americans. These people weren't wealthy or famous.

But as a photographer, Dorothea strived to capture their true spirit and dignity.

In 1925, Dorothea gave birth to their first son. The couple named him Daniel Rhodes Dixon. Three years later, they welcomed another son. They named him John Eaglefeather Dixon.

Most of the time Maynard would be away from home. Dorothea was left to take care of the house and their boys. She was torn between work and spending time with her sons. Often she would ask friends to keep an

Dorothea took this photograph of Maynard Dixon with their two sons, John and Daniel.

eye on the boys. But it was never easy for Dorothea to be away from her children.

In 1929, the family visited the California countryside. One afternoon Dorothea headed off by herself. She got caught in a powerful storm. The rain poured down. The wind blew hard. Dorothea sat on a large rock to rest. She thought about which of her photographs were most pleasing to her. At that moment something became very clear to Dorothea. It didn't matter if her subjects were wealthy or poor. Someday she would photograph all kinds of people.

> " Right in the middle of it, with the thunder bursting and the wind whistling, it came to me that what I had to do was to take pictures and concentrate upon people, only people, all kinds of people, people who paid me and people who didn't, "
>
> said Dorothea Lange, recalling her experience being stranded during a storm.

CHAPTER 4
Change of Direction

On October 29, 1929, the U.S. stock market crashed. Soon many businesses closed. Millions of Americans had no jobs. The country was in the middle of the Great Depression. Many Americans didn't have money

This photograph, taken by Dorothea Lange, shows out-of-work men standing on line to receive unemployment checks.

to buy food. Many couldn't pay for their homes, either. These people were forced to live with family members or to live on the streets.

Dorothea and her family struggled, too. The couple still had their home and money to buy what their family needed. However, the two were beginning to find it more difficult to sell their art.

By 1930, more businesses had closed and many more people were out of work. Some banks had shut their doors, too. Life was getting very difficult for everyone.

> . . . we were confronted with the terrors of the Depression. Not that we didn't have enough to eat, but everyone was so shocked and panicky. No one knew what was ahead,
>
> said Dorothea, describing San Francisco during the start of the Great Depression.

Dorothea and Maynard now realized that they needed to begin making changes. People had stopped buying Maynard's paintings. Dorothea's customers had stopped scheduling portraits. The couple still had money for food. However, they had to sell their home.

Painting was important to Maynard. And photography was very important to Dorothea. Maynard was away from home often. Dorothea would be left to take care of the household. Because of this, there was little time for photography. This caused many arguments between the couple. Soon they agreed it would be best for them to part ways.

By 1932, one in every four Americans had lost their job. One way the government and generous citizens tried to help was by providing the jobless with free meals. Hundreds of men stood in lines called breadlines. When it was their turn, they were given a bowl of thin soup and a piece of bread. It wasn't much. But it was better than nothing.

One day Dorothea glanced out of her studio's window. A long line of ragtag men stood outside. They were waiting to be served a meal. A wealthy woman had donated the food. People called her "The White Angel."

Dorothea was overcome with emotion. She recalled the thoughts she'd had when she was caught in the storm. She had vowed that someday she would photograph people with all sorts of lives. Now was her chance.

Dorothea's concern for people in trouble and her passion for photography took over. She ran outside with her camera. Soon she found herself in the middle of the crowd. It was scary on the street. The men were unhappy. They were also hungry and frustrated. Dorothea knew she had to be careful. She didn't want to make the men even more upset.

Dorothea thought back to her childhood. She recalled the many times she had walked alone through the streets of New York City. Dorothea thought about how she had made herself invisible. The lessons she had learned paid off again. Unnoticed, Dorothea began taking pictures.

> This was a preparation, hard as it was, but it was a preparation,
>
> said Dorothea, reflecting on her late-night walks through New York City's streets.

One photograph Dorothea took on that day became famous. It's called *White Angel Breadline*. Most of the men in the photograph have their backs to the camera. But one man's face is visible. The rim of his dirty hat shields

White Angel Breadline, 1933

his eyes. He wears a grim and sorrowful expression. His arms rest on the fence. His hands are clasped in front of him holding an empty tin cup.

In *White Angel Breadline*, Dorothea exposed the emotions that the man felt. People could see his sadness, anger, and concern. The photograph forced people to wonder about the man. Was he scared? Was he praying the food wouldn't run out? People now understood that others were suffering because of the Great Depression.

> I can only say I knew I was looking at something [important],
>
> said Dorothea Lange about taking the photograph *White Angel Breadline*.

Soon Dorothea returned to the streets with her camera. She'd photograph a demonstration at San Francisco's Civic Center. Thousands of people had gathered there. Many of them carried large signs. The workers were angry. They were protesting against a lack of jobs.

Dorothea knew she was in the middle of a dangerous scene. Again she made herself invisible. On this day, she

took another famous photograph, *General Strike/Street Meeting, San Francisco*. The subject of the photograph is a policeman. A star shines on his chest. The emblem is a symbol of his power. He seems unconcerned about the feelings of the demonstrators.

General Strike/Street Meeting, San Francisco,
Dorothea Lange, 1933

Dorothea didn't know what to do with the pictures she had taken. So she decorated her walls with the images. Now she was taking portraits of the helpless and needy. Her photographs told stories of poverty, worry, anger, and hopelessness. They were examples of what was happening to people all over America. These people couldn't pay her. Regardless, she knew the portraits were important.

> I never had any sense in making a career out of it. It was more a sense of personal commitment,
>
> Dorothea said about her decision to take street photography.

Soon Willard Van Dyke saw a sample of her street photographs. Willard was a photographer and a friend of Dorothea's. He owned a small art gallery. In 1934, Willard decided to host a display of Dorothea's work.

The gallery show was a success. People who attended the exhibit were enlightened. Dorothea's images helped viewers understand that the Great Depression created

huge problems for many people. Viewers gained a new awareness of the hardships that many Americans were experiencing.

A university professor named Paul Taylor visited Dorothea's exhibit. He was very moved by the young woman's photographs. Paul had spent the last 10 years reporting about the life of California's poor farmers. He soon learned that he and Dorothea had the same goal. They both wished to expose the story of the poor in America.

Paul realized that Dorothea's photographs would add meaning and power to his written reports. He asked if she would be interested in helping with his projects. Dorothea knew that working with Paul would be a great opportunity for her. Now she would be able to use her talent to help people.

CHAPTER 5
On a Mission

By the early 1930s, thousands of farmers in the Midwest and on the Great Plains were facing hardships. Most had thought they'd get through the Great Depression with little struggle. But soon disaster struck.

To make money, farmers had over planted. They covered every acre of their land with wheat. This used up the minerals in the soil. Soon many new crops wouldn't grow. Then from 1930 to 1936, droughts hit the Great Plains. Crops died from the lack of rain. Strong winds that are common across the Midwest took over. Huge clouds of dirt filled the sky. Little rainfall combined with the heavy winds caused the topsoil to blow away. This event became known as the Dust Bowl.

Soon the farmers couldn't grow crops. Meanwhile, news was spreading about the large number of jobs that could be found planting and harvesting farmland in

A farm about to be enveloped by a dust storm during the Dust Bowl of the 1930s.

California. Farm families felt they had no choice but to head west.

Many farmers had no car and no money. They headed for California on foot. Those who had a car loaded it with any belongings they could. Then they motored west.

The farmers' journeys took months. Finally they would make it to California. Thousands of farmers were pouring into the state. There were now more people in California than there were jobs. So finding work wasn't

Dorothea Lange photographed this Midwestern family, all packed up and ready for the long road trip to California. (detail of the photograph called *Dust Bowl Refugees Reach a "Promised Land"-California/"A Family Unit in the Flight From Drought"*, 1936 is pictured)

easy. The farmers became migrant workers. They moved from farm to farm as different crops became ready to plant and pick.

In the 1930s, most of California's crops were planted and harvested by hand. Harvesting crops in the California sunshine was a very difficult way to make money. The work took much physical effort. Workers were often paid by how many crops they picked. This meant they had to work as fast as they could.

Life in California was much different than in the Midwest or on the Great Plains. Most families lived

Migrant workers spent many hours bent over in the fields. The work was uncomfortable and often backbreaking.

in large tents. Their makeshift camps had no running water. There weren't any bathrooms, and there was no electricity. All they had to eat was the crop they were picking at the time.

In 1934, Paul Taylor was given a new assignment. The government asked him to investigate why farmers from the Midwest and Great Plains were moving to California. The State Emergency Relief Administration (SERA) wanted Paul's advice on how to address the situation.

Paul convinced SERA to hire Dorothea as well. They agreed she could work for one month. Paul hoped that Dorothea's photographs would be good. Then maybe SERA would hire her for longer.

> " . . . this shaking off of people from their own roots [which] started with those big storms, and it was like a movement of the earth, . . . "
>
> said Dorothea Lange about the farmers' migration to the west.

In 1935, Dorothea and Paul traveled to Southern California. They recorded the living conditions of the migrant workers. The goal of their report was to expose the workers' problems. They hoped they could convince the government to provide the families with aid.

The two started work at 6 A.M. each day. Paul interviewed farmers and their families. Dorothea took their pictures. The assignment was rough. But Paul was driven. The two worked well together. They both wanted to open people's eyes to the problems of the poor in America.

A Texas family of seven lived in this tent. Photographs like this one, taken by Dorothea in California, provided the FSA with a clear picture of how terrible the migrant workers' living conditions really were.

Dorothea was shocked by the conditions in the migrant worker camps. Many of the homes were overcrowded. The workers' living spaces were dirty, too. Their homes were crude and pitiful.

In each of her photographs, Dorothea wanted the people's dignity to shine through. So she spent much time with the migrant workers. She interviewed them, just as she had with her wealthy clients. She wanted to get to know the families. In this way, Dorothea was able to earn their trust.

The migrant workers sensed Dorothea cared very much about their problems. When she limped toward them with her camera, they were at ease. They could tell Dorothea had experienced hardship, too.

> You know, so often it's just sticking around and being there, remaining there, not swooping in and swooping out in a cloud of dust, sitting down on the ground with people, letting children look at your camera, . . .
>
> Dorothea Lange said, describing how she approached her subjects.

The image of this child, taken by Dorothea Lange in 1936, showed people the hardships and extreme poverty experienced by Midwesterners during the Dust Bowl. (photograph called *Child Living in an Oklahoma City Shacktown* is pictured)

Soon Paul and Dorothea returned to San Francisco. They gave their work to SERA. The report had a huge impact. SERA shared the work with the Farm Security Administration (FSA). This government agency worked to find ways to help poor farmers. After reviewing the report, the FSA gave Dorothea's photographs to newspapers and magazines. Now people everywhere would see how poor migrant workers were treated. Soon afterwards the government began to build decent camps for the farm families.

Dorothea has fun photographing a migrant worker's child.

Dorothea liked that her photographs had changed people's lives. She wanted to photograph more people in trouble. Dorothea felt it was important to bring attention to critical situations. Now she knew she could do this successfully through photography. Work like this became known as photojournalism. Dorothea was positive that this was the work she was meant to do.

"

I had to get my camera to register the things about those people that were more important than how poor they were—their pride, their strength, their spirit,"

Dorothea Lange said, explaining her goals when photographing migrant farm workers.

Soon Dorothea closed her portrait studio. She continued to work with Paul. As the year went by, the two fell in love. They were married in December 1935.

In 1936, the FSA hired Dorothea as a photographer. This time she went to Southern California alone. She drove through the countryside to find migrant workers and camps to photograph.

Dorothea and Paul Taylor during one of their
projects with the FSA

In the spring, Dorothea had finished one of her
assignments. She was tired. A cold rain was falling as
she drove home. She happened to pass a crude sign. It
read, "Pea Picker's Camp." Dorothea drove on. But then
suddenly she decided to turn back. Something inside her
told her to investigate the camp.

Dorothea's instincts paid off. At the camp she found
a group of cold, hungry workers. Farmers were gathered

in makeshift tents. The shelters were held up with tree branches. Dorothea noticed a woman under one of the tents with several small children.

Dorothea limped towards the tent, pausing to take photographs of the family as she got closer. One of these pictures, called *Migrant Mother*, would become the most famous of Dorothea's career. In the picture, the woman stares off into the distance. Feelings of worry and despair flood her face. The mother's burdens seem overwhelming. On her arm lies a baby. Dirt covers its face. Her young children cling to her sides. They are dirty, too.

"I saw and approached the hungry and desperate mother, as if drawn by a magnet. There she sat in that lean-to tent with her children huddled around her, and seemed to know that my picture might help her, and so she helped me,"

Dorothea Lange later wrote about her experience at the pea picker's camp.

Dorothea never asked the woman her name. But she did learn about the problems the farmers were having.

Florence Owens Thompson was the subject of Dorothea Lange's famous photograph called *Migrant Mother*, taken in 1936. (photograph called *Migrant Mother*, is pictured)

The pea crop had frozen. This was because of the unusual cold. Sometimes they'd catch a bird or squirrel for food. But for the most part, all they had to eat were frozen peas.

Dorothea knew that the photographs she had taken at the pea picker's camp were all the FSA needed to see. The next day she took her work to the *San Francisco News*. The newspaper quickly put together her story. Soon the article and her photographs were printed in newspapers across the country.

Dorothea's photographs from the pea picker's camp upset Americans. Many couldn't believe that the people who provided them with food had nothing to eat themselves. Soon the government sent tons of food to the migrant workers. Dorothea's work had made a difference.

That summer Dorothea and Paul took off on another assignment. They drove through the Great Plains, the Deep South, and the American Southwest. Again their goal was to expose poor people's suffering.

On this trip, Dorothea took another well-known photograph called, *Plantation Overseer and His Field Hands*. It illustrates the relationship between a landowner and poor farmers. In the photograph, a

landowner rests his foot on the bumper of his shiny new car. Behind him are five thin African American men. It's clear the landowner benefits from the hard work the men do.

By the end of the summer, the couple had traveled more than 17,000 miles. They decided to write a book about their work. *American Exodus: A Record of Human Erosion* was published in 1939. Book critics called it a masterpiece of photojournalism.

Plantation Overseer and His Field Hands, 1936

CHAPTER 6
Hurdles

By the end of 1939, the Great Depression was over. And the year also brought an end to Dorothea's job with the FSA. But the talented photographer's work was far from over. The Bureau of Agricultural Economics (BAE) hired Dorothea in 1941. Her job was to photograph farm life in California and Arizona. The work was similar to what she had done for the FSA.

Around this time Dorothea and Paul moved to Berkeley, California. Their new house sat on top of a hill. Big oak trees surrounded it. The yard had a large garden with flowers that bloomed throughout the year. Dorothea built a studio and a darkroom in the backyard.

In 1941, the Japanese attacked Pearl Harbor. The United States then entered World War II. At that time many Japanese people lived on America's West Coast. The American people were suspicious of this group of citizens. They wondered if Japanese Americans could be trusted.

Dorothea Lange took this photograph of young
Japanese Americans traveling to internment camps.

In February 1942, President Franklin D. Roosevelt
ordered that all Japanese Americans be sent to relocation
centers. More than 100,000 people were forced to leave
their homes. The people could take with them only what
they could carry. They were sent to live at internment
camps. The Japanese Americans didn't know it at the time,
but they would be confined in the camps for four years.

In 1942, the War Relocation Authority (WRA) hired Dorothea. They wanted her to photograph Japanese Americans being moved to camps. Dorothea worked long hours. She traveled to and from the Northern California camps each day.

Most Americans approved of the government's action. But Dorothea was outraged. She felt it wasn't right to force these American citizens to live in camps. She believed the government was taking away the

Dorothea Lange is pictured with her camera, surrounded by a crowd of Japanese Americans en route to the internment camps.

Japanese American's freedom. By agreeing to do this job, Dorothea knew that she could show others that the government was being unfair.

The WRA knew how Dorothea felt about the camps. They watched her closely. She wasn't allowed to take pictures of the barbed wire that surrounded the camps. She also couldn't photograph the watchtowers or guards that patrolled the grounds during the day and at night. When Dorothea was finished with the project, the WRA took her photographs away. Dorothea's pictures from the camps weren't seen by the public until after the war had ended.

World War II caused much sadness for all Americans. But the war did help the country, too. Fifteen million Americans were serving in the military. This caused a shortage of workers at home. Many women joined the work force. Thousands of migrant workers were now able to find jobs. Suddenly, everyone who could work was needed.

All kind of work sprang up. The military needed equipment and uniforms. So people were hired to make clothing and supplies. Ships were needed to move items overseas. Soon many people were given jobs on docks.

Dorothea took this picture of the American flag flying high over
the Manzanar, California Internment Camp.

Dorothea Lange took this picture titled, *Women Line Up for Paychecks-Richmond Shipyards*, in 1942.

All of a sudden there were more jobs than there were people. It was the beginning of a prosperous time for America.

In 1944, *Fortune* magazine hired Dorothea. They wanted her to take photographs of the busy shipyards in Richmond, California. The location had become the biggest shipbuilding center in the world.

Fortune hired another well-known photographer to work with Dorothea. His name was Ansel Adams. The two had very different approaches to their work. Ansel liked to capture large scenes. He was best known for his panoramic images of Western landscapes. For this assignment he chose to capture the grandness of the ships in the harbor. Dorothea stayed true to her own photographic style, too. She took portraits of the dockworkers.

World War II ended in 1945. Dorothea was now 40 years old. During the next five years she dealt with different health problems. She would need to rest. However, Dorothea didn't abandon her cameras. She used them to take photographs around her home. Photography played too big a part in Dorothea's life. She wasn't about to give it up.

CHAPTER 7
A Visual Life

In 1951, Dorothea spoke at a national photography conference. She shared her views about photojournalism. She revealed three rules that she had made for herself: hands off, place, and time. Hands off meant she wouldn't pose her subjects. Place stressed that she would photograph people as part of their natural environment. She believed this helped viewers understand the picture. Her last rule, time, was based on her belief that photographs should clearly reflect the times and conditions in which they were taken.

Some photographers at the conference decided to start a magazine. It would be called *Aperture*. Dorothea and Ansel Adams were co-founders of the publication. The first issue was printed in 1952. The magazine is still published today.

When Dorothea returned to California, she worked on a project of her own called, "To a Cabin." She and

Following the rules of photojournalism that she had made for herself, Dorothea captured the true emotions of a migrant worker's young daughter. (photograph called *Girl Leaning on a Fence*, 1939 is pictured)

Paul had bought a small cabin. It overlooked the Pacific Ocean. Dorothea photographed her children and grandchildren when they visited there. This was one of her favorite projects.

In 1958, Paul was hired to study farm communities in Asia, South America, and the Middle East. He'd be away for a very long time. Dorothea went on the trip with her husband and took many photographs. After they returned home a year later, the couple received bad news. Dorothea had cancer.

Shortly after she learned of her illness, the Museum of Modern Art in New York City contacted Dorothea. They wanted her to set up a one-woman exhibit. This was a huge honor. Dorothea was the first woman photographer to be invited to do a show at the museum. Despite her fragile health, she felt it was important that she share her photographs with others.

> A photographer's files are in a sense his autobiography. More resides there than he is aware of,
>
> said Dorothea Lange.

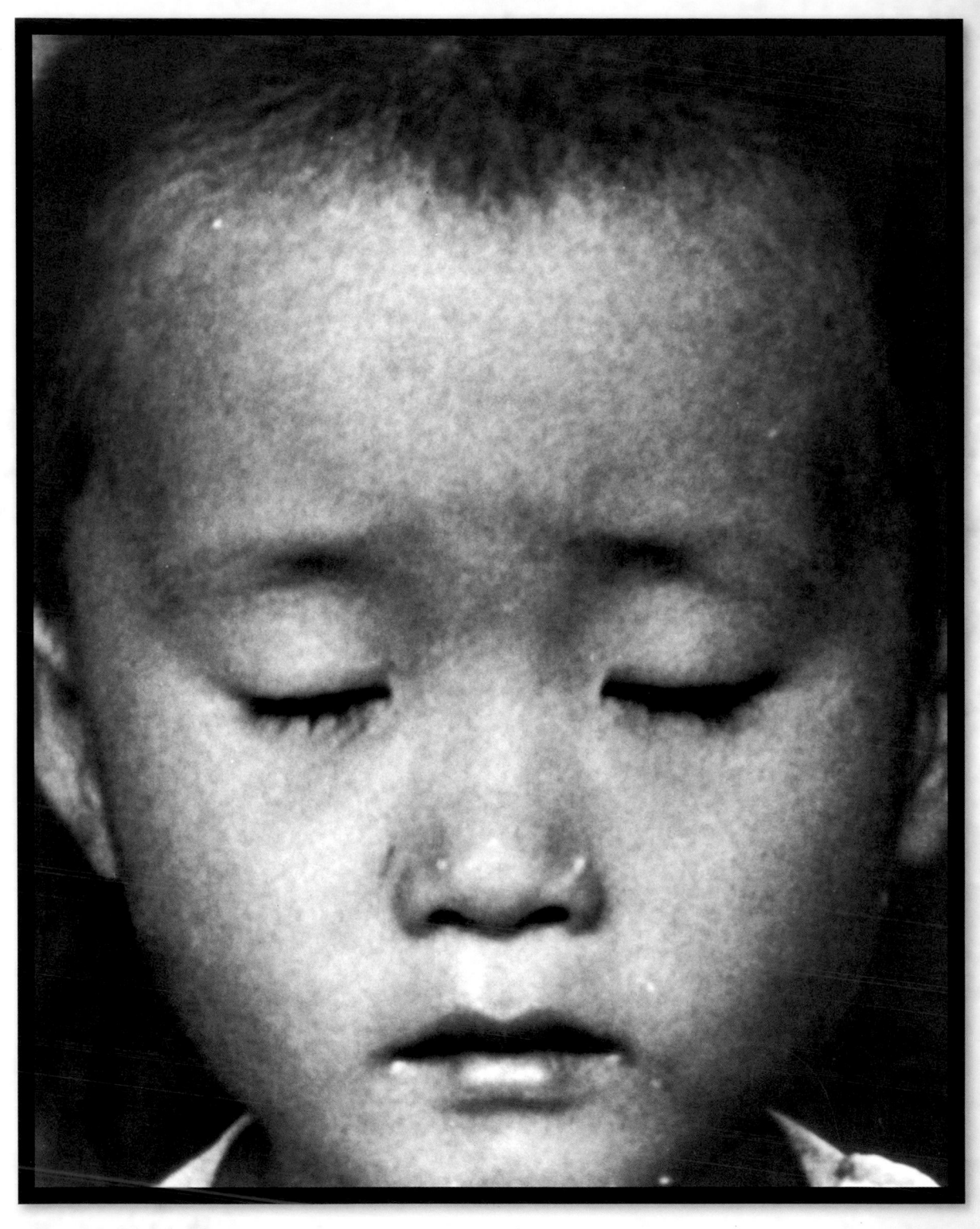

On a trip to Asia in 1958, Dorothea took this photograph called *Korean Child*. It is one of the last well-known photographs she took.

Dorothea Lange, circa 1960

It took months to prepare for the exhibit. Dorothea looked through her files. She had taken over 10,000 photographs over 40 years. Dorothea mixed pictures she'd taken while traveling with photographs of her family. The final exhibit contained 200 images.

Dorothea Lange died on October 11, 1965. She was 70 years old. Dorothea was a pioneer in photojournalism. Her camera told many tales. Beginning with photographs of victims of the Great Depression, her purpose had become clear. She realized that she could use her talent to send a message. During her lifetime, Dorothea touched the lives of thousands. Her images will continue to stir people's emotions for ages to come.

"One should really use the camera as though tomorrow you'd be stricken blind. To live a visual life is an enormous undertaking, practically unattainable. I have only touched it, just touched it,"

Dorothea Lange said about her photography career.

Glossary

breadline a line of people waiting to receive free food

darkroom a room with little or no light where photographers develop film and print photographs

dignity (1) a sense of pride in oneself (2) the state or quality of being worthy of self respect

demonstration a public meeting or march protesting something or expressing views on a political issue

exhibit to display artwork in a gallery or a museum

frame (1) surround so as to create a sharp or attractive image (2) a case or border enclosing a picture

film a thin flexible strip of plastic or other material coated with light-sensitive chemicals for exposure in a camera, used to produce photographs or motion pictures

gallery a room or building used to display or sell works of art

immigrant a person who comes to live permanently in a foreign country

internment camp a place where a specific group of people are confined for political or military reasons

migrant worker person moving from one region of a country to another to find work

panoramic a picture or photograph containing a wide view

photographer a person who takes photographs as a hobby or to earn a living

polio a highly infectious viral disease that may attack the central nervous system and is characterized by symptoms that range from an infection to total loss of the ability to move a part or parts of the body in a matter of hours

portrait a painting, drawing, photograph, or engraving of a person, especially one depicting only the face or head and shoulders

poverty the state of being extremely poor

proof first prints of a photograph

shipyard a place where ships are built and repaired

studio a room where a photographer or other artists work

subject a person or thing that is the focus of a photograph or piece of art